ANTIPHONAL AIRS

ANTIPHONAL AIRS

Joseph Noble

SKYLIGHT PRESS

© Joseph Noble 2013

First published in Great Britain in 2013 by Skylight Press,
210 Brooklyn Road, Cheltenham, Glos GL51 8EA

Joseph Noble has asserted his right to be identified as the author of
this work.

Cover artwork: 'Filament' by Brian Lucas
Designed and typeset by Rebsie Fairholm
Publisher: Daniel Staniforth

www.skylightpress.co.uk

Printed and bound in Great Britain by Lightning Source, Milton
Keynes

Typeset in Mrs Eaves 13/16pt, a font by Zuzana Licko. Titles set in
Orpheus Pro, a font by Canada Type.

British Library Cataloguing-in-Publication data: a catalogue record
for this book is available from the British Library.

ISBN 978-1-908011-64-0

Contents

Invenzioni e Stravaganze

"Wonders Upon a Note"

Nicola Matteis, London, 1676-1687

the music is forgotten
caught in the air above water
span strung a hand's breadth

the foot steps across the border

over the waves
an unknown music
rushes at us

the past a clamour
a music unidentifiable

the tree cut, sawed, shaped
into neck, belly, ribs
a foreign tree
an unknown body
held at the edge of breath
by the fingers
sounding what it is not
that it is

a wondering note
questions the air:
a hand disappearing

the waves rush at us
knowledge a noise
we don't understand yet

the fingers never touched the hairs
that touched the strings
bowing "as from the clouds"
ayre to air

Antiphonal Effects

Dario Castello, Venice, 1621-1629

I

read what
is not written
but heard

an echo history
voiced in antiphony
between brick and water

an unwritten biography
inscribed by voices
in colloquy

from bridge to bridge
cello matching violin
notes mirrored

above water
what is not written
is sounded between

and each time
is played
through times

II

scratch built

in air and water

hears itself

in a name

drawn through

sound holes

whispers through

canals and streets

where note

quickened steps

echo between

what is not

discovered

Passacaglio

Biagio Marini; Venice, Brescia, Neuburg, Düsseldorf, Brussels, Ferrara, Milan, Vicenza, Venice; 1615-1663

a violin string across the alps
your feet scatter their steps
then bring them home
"senza cadenza"

inventive love
turns in mid-stream
reconsiders
re-turns, hesitates
changes its shape
("e che vuoi da me?")

a passage halfway there
passamezzo
two single steps forward
one double step back

"the obscurity of these few notes"
in the mouth, on the string

curious love
tests the air
listens for an echo

and response
held in the air
and dying on the ears

the tune turns
and the steps pass

the stubborn rhythm
is mouthed at the lips

withdraws mute
a curious echo

listening
to be heard

passing
in the street

La Trasformata

Marco Uccellini; Modena, Parma; 1639-1680

the little bird
leaves no trace
no claw prints
no call
no echo
little more than
a potato print
on the page
"per servire
ad un amico"
who looks for signs

finch caught in the wind:
air thrust from its own melody
mouth that moves toward silence or song
transforming what is unseen into what is heard
what is unheard into what is imagined

little bird, beautiful bird
how ever do you know
how to compose so well
a song hiding in the air
forgetting its own name

little bird, beautiful bird
how ever do you know
how to trace so well
scratches that outline the notes
with the whisper of a name

little bird, beautiful bird
how ever do you know
how to keep silence so well
holding a name so long
until it becomes a song

a bird
not yet a bird
a bird
yet not a bird
dust already
and dust ready
at hand
had and hadn't
halved
holed throat
swallowing stones
note by note
ground
and turned
to dust
loosed
yet tuned
to dust
the whole throat
not yet
already singing

uccellino,
air forgets its name
(water upon the sun)

a fever fingers syllables
(ink spilling its reins)

uccellino,
harp in the street
(who turns the sun?)

song wheel in the iris
(swallow dilating sleep)

uccellino,
river flings itself into its reflection
(drum collides with the wind)

air is shaping the ear
(map on the tympanum)

uccellino,
angel climbs through the arm
(which finch in the ankle?)

Altri Istromenti

Giovanni Battista Fontana; Brescia, Rome, Venice, Padua;
1610-1641

translated through wood
voices break out from the chorus
and rise from the ends of strings

what translation occurs from
hand to page to hand
to wood to ear?

what affection dwells there
between melody and flesh
at the taut string's boundary?

divine the shorthand

passaggi e affetti

what moves

is touch upon a tone

stone turned to ear

bass figured into waves
scales slip through the hands

the music in hand
blows from the mouth

through the conical bore
la bora figures the waves

riding a birth pressing against the ears'
shells hearing the waves

that have entered them
and through which they move

with the body's swaying staves
touching upon the air quickened by

the music rising from two sticks
rubbed together by the hands

Capricci

Girolamo Frescobaldi; Ferrara, Rome, Brussels, Rome, Mantua,
Rome, Florence, Rome; 1597-1643

Safe, sound, and happy, I arrived in Rome,
October 29, 1608, on the eve of All Saint's Day
and took possession of the organ at St. Peter's.
From then on I could be found all over –
from chapels to cardinals' apartments –
and on any number of instruments.
Enzo tried to arrange a marriage for me
to Caccini's daughter, and Caccini countered
with an even more generous offer:
his daughter's hand and employment for both
Enzo and I in Florence, with very little duties.
But I stayed in Rome.
Oh, yes, there was that little indiscretion with
Angiolina, a year or so after I arrived.
And then Francesco was born before Orsola and I
married, but we eventually did, and then came
Maddalena, Domenico, Stefano, and Caterina.
Well, that's how I went about things.
They say I'm uncouth and unschooled,
but musicians come to me from all over Europe
to be schooled. And I guess I'm good enough
for the Inquisitor of Malta to baptize Caterina,
and my dedication to Cardinal Borghese
was not taken as uncouth, nor the works as unschooled.
Oh, Doni had an axe to grind,
a little man working for the great Barberini
(these private secretaries are always this way),
but anyone who looks at even my early madrigals
can see how I worked them to the words.

In my first book of toccatas, I say there that
madrigals should be performed with a flexible beat
"according to the emotions aroused or
the meaning of the words that are sung."
All the little man had to do was open his eyes
and read. Opening his ears would have helped too.
So, if I get overly involved in my music
and have no patience for people at times,
well, so be it. Listen to the music.
That's where I put everything. If I seem
a bit uncouth at times, that's because
you can find more of me at the tip
of my fingers than at the tip of my tongue.
Luzzaschi taught me well, and I worked hard.
And so I didn't need a silvery tongue.
The patronage followed anyway, drawn by the music.

Relations with Enzo cooled, so on to Aldobrandini.
The old Brand tried to burn me, but, ha!,
I showed him what I was made of,
and took him to court. Take my house, indeed!
And it was a wedding gift from Orsola's father.
For three years I worked for the Aldobrandinis.
Yes, I then tried Mantua, right after Monteverdi left,
but those Gonzaga's were impossible.
Monteverdi found that out, and so did I.
So back to Rome after only three months.
Yet, St. Peter's paid me the whole time.
So, for the next thirteen years, more or less,
I settled again into things in Rome.
Vincenti reprinted the ricercares and canzonas
as well as the first book of caprices.
No dedication and no patron's money needed.
I guess you could say I was doing all right.

Yes, I learned much from Luzzaschi
and those others in Ferrara, as well as
those Neapolitans like Macque and Trabaci
that d'Este brought to court. Old Alfonso would
listen to music everyday for two to four hours.
That was a place to learn!
There was still so much in the old music,
weaving those voices together,
and I could see how one could yet
carry it to such fruition, and still
bring in the new work that drew
out the single voice into its own.
I loved to draw that voice out and
see where it would lead, spinning it out on a dare,
and then bring back the other voices
that would imitate or echo or rework it.
It was such fun! Which way did I look,
they wondered, forwards or backwards? Ha!
It was such fun, spinning it all out on a dare!
In the caprices, the listener cannot help
marvelling at besides delighting in the music.

In 1628, I dedicated my first book of canzonas
to Ferdinando II de' Medici, and in November
of that same year St. Peter's granted me a leave
of absence to go to the Florentine court.
Florence was fine, but uneventful.
I brought out a book of musical airs,
nothing complex, but songs in which
the voice can take delight.
Then old Rome lured me back
with an offer from the Barberinis.

I guess I am now a grand old man.
Students come to me from all over Europe.
Froberger has been studying with me
for about two years now.
I came out with a book of musical flowers
and revised my first book of toccatas,
adding some new pieces. Some are simpler,
some more complex than earlier works;
some look forward, some back.
Della Valle says there are more
'gallantries' in my new work.
Do you think so? I don't know.
What does it matter what people say?
I continue composing; though lately,
I haven't even published many of my pieces.
I just enjoy writing them. Let him who is able
understand me; I understand myself.

Solfeggio

*Giovanni Bonaventura Viviani; Italy, Austria, Germany, Italy;
1656-1693*

off the cuff
and onto the bow
from chapel to chamber
doves, beak to beak

Florence, Innsbruck, Augsburg...

a boy in a cuckoo's nest
whistles through a clock
the sky looks for a name
following the year

Venice, Rome, Naples...

a quill conducts the archangel
in camera to the church
the impresario flees his creditors
cypresses for feet

Milan, Naples again...

the stage remembers steps and songs
confusions of comings and goings
beaks holding cicadas
maranzzanos wiggling umbilici

Calabria, Pistoia...

losing trace until this time
each time, two voices study
the textless syllables, singing
the last things they know

Madrigal

Claudio Monteverdi; Cremona, Mantua, Venice; 1582-1643

though we do not hear the song
we listen to it
the voices move between each other
the beak cracks the seed husk
so the eyelids open
the sparrow is at my ear

she whom I loved has died
but my love continues to live
I would both be silent and sing
it is not pain that transforms me
but recognition —
that my voice comes from my own throat
that my heart beats in my own chest
that this is the moment each moment

lips circle breath
through which they kiss
the air she no longer breathes
finger strums pendulum
the head tilts back and
her voice is there, at the mouth

Capriccio Stravagante

Carlo Farina; Mantua, Dresden, Torgau, Parma, Massa, Danzig, Italy; 1625-1640

there is no return, only a song
drawn along the strings
remembering
what she wishes to forget
which she listens to
to remember

lip step   rill harp
a worm a wound a wing
tooth a vein of quartz
soil scratching its back
dog before the gate
water scraping a living

no rings in the sun
a ripening orientation
faces drawn from breath

shadow clang
a point in space
rattling a cage

what she asks
I can only imagine
and imagining I ask
and asking I picture
what she is
asking to imagine
that I am thinking
which she says
thinking we do
what we imagine
as and is
as an is

season is partly while
in its own prosperity
something again for hidden

bell skin reaching limb
aloud tensile
letters' conversant migration

mouth pulled over grin —
walk with no trace of walking —
shroud bird's fragile gears —
flame its own mirror — name and
breath double-stop common time

digging in the earth —
drumming —
a cup at the lips

syntax is scoured and omitted
consonants live at the edge
of sickle and shovel

the earth is known
only through mouths

sentience dilates
its pores

the teeth's commerce
creates the body

❧

he found himself on a street
where he knew the names of nothing

so much so that he could not
compare one thing to another

it was all birdsong to him
the sole metaphor he could think of

sound without naming
meaning without naming

he saw each thing
as he heard it

each and own self
void emblem

❧

to find her
I follow her silence
and follow instead
nothing said

nothing heard
follows her lips
slips within
a word she says

a word she sings
follows her tongue
quivering within
a silence sung

not because he couldn't find himself
but because he couldn't hear himself

it was within a space
constructed for his voice

throat that had been described
to him before he had a body
word before he had lips

the nothing that he was
inhabited the air as
something or other

identical as alike
equal as just

a temperament singing
an interval from itself

Trio Sonata

Salomone Rossi; Mantua; 1607-1622

that they are
what they are
singing and
singing sung

each of two
to one
hums a sum
one at a time
played together

within the space set aside
within the sound
within the space that sounds
within the tune
within the hand that places

there that
that is are
two become one
become two again
four become three
though still four

each guitar,
basso, dibraccio
fiddle faces
space to line
space to live
place within pace:
passage work

umbilical bell
dangles feet
the ear scrolls
the neck and
drawn across
the belly the hand
clears a path

that they are
what they are
sung and
sung singing

Sonata Sonetto

Giovanni Legrenzi; Bergamo, Ferrara, Venice; 1655-1690

the name's melancholy
the name's memory
before any extravagance of the future
the name softens the blow

it realizes a dead language
its typography creates its own fantasia
the page's delirium
the bee's mouth

the name strikes out on its own
carries a honeycomb in its belly
pulls a string across the turtle's shell
runs its fingers along the sky's bell

the name calls what is unknown
out of what is known

The Mask's Name

Sigismondo D'India, "Nobile Palermitano"; Naples, Mantua,
Parma, Venice, Florence, Rome, Turin, Modena; 1606-1624

Dorinda to Silvio

That eyes would hear and ears see:
each sense not making sense but for
the logic of its sensing your presence:
fingers tasting what tongues would touch:
a word's scent sent from your lips to
an unknown sense listening from that part
of me I cannot pinpoint but which stirs
in a body I do not know that I live in.
Your word sounds in colloquy with a word
I had forgotten but now hear from these my own
awakening lips, bringing to life that discovered
body else lain dormant, which now, seeing
sense, hears that which it knows to be
and living itself now, lives to know.

Silvio to Dorinda

You refuse that which is yours, what you have
won; the years I held you distant, when the prize
of my solitary freedom held my gaze,
were a muddied clarity, an open-eyed wandering
through what I didn't see. Hear and see how
your voice became an image I could no longer
be deaf to, how your vision filled my ears and ringing
before me moved the air to incarnate your body.
Do not turn now from that which you have conjured:
this body you have created to recognize
your own. It has forgotten itself in touching you,
has forgotten its being in being with you;
do not forget him who found himself in forgetting
his unlived life by choosing our life to live.

Dorinda and Silvio to Sigismondo

the voices at once

        who even by your name

naming what you would become

        you saw and saw not

            neither severally nor...

and singly heard upon the string

        stretched across each silence

you would broach in approaching

            the air to give you back your soul

neither known nor not known

        two foreign names

from the native land

        the mask found in the hands

inhabited breath

        breathed into

        who you would become

naming what you saw

        and saw not

        stretched across the silence

Opus 3 x 4

Giovanni Antonio Pandolfi Mealli; Innsbruck, Messina?; 1660-1669

La Stella

what is known
happens in the steps
to the dance
six of one
half dozen of another

twelve names on the lips
sunlight at the hand

a loom, a bow
"stylus phantasticus"
coronal threads
humming with the
rogue's dialect

La Cesta

a box filled with missing diaries and letters
a box filled with what is chewed away by mice
a box filled with absent memoirs
a box filled with manuscripts not found
a box sunk to the bottom of the Danube
a box blown into the straits of Messina
a box filled with an invented name
a box awaiting rediscovery
a box filled with an invented past
a box filled with what little can be proven
a box filled with what little can be disproved
a box filled with nothing else

La Melana

beside the eggplant sits
an orange half in light
the crimson of the apple
becomes rose in full sun

the purple, oblong bottle
stands behind the eggplant
which lays flat and at whose
left side rests a green-yellow pear

the table cloth reveals
the names of fruit while
a geranium peers from behind
a vase adjoining the apple

La Castella

from room to room
walking a round
there's no place like

where you hang your hat
your head dreams through
room to room

remembers a name
walking a round
end to end

up on your head
a round horizon
dreaming a hat

La Clemente

the past is the past
and the present gives us clemency
at the twelfth hour

a history found in a whisper

untitled original
discovered among fiddle sticks
scratching out a sound

a whisper found in a name

respite taken in a finger
dancing on a string
are you lost and gone forever?

a name found in a tune

La Sabbatina

leaves still
in cold
grey light
at hand
turns knob
while step
rests in
path strung
as you go
along the
sand humming
a name

La Bernabea

steps to a name
trippingly over its own
slip of a history

who'd have thought
a single mention
free to invent
so few instructions

an educated instinct —
ankle or wrist joint
making the movement
of bone and muscle possible
through a space between

La Viviana

Name got his palm read: the forecast was not good.
All of his children would be illegitimate;
none would answer to him. He would be recognized
for only a short time; indeed, the palmist had already
forgotten whose future he was foretelling.

In order to survive, Name found sustenance
on others' lips and fed on air:
he started as a rumbling in the belly,
worked his way up to tickle the bronchia,
quivered in the throat, plucked the vocal cords,
shivered, and spun da capo from a mouth
leaving an echo behind to be found in the air.

La Monella Romanesca

both faces give direct glances
honesty in duplicity
this is the law of the street
a moveable spine
and a hard external skeleton

remember what you say and
don't let what you say be known
a word is transfixed in its own deflection
be remembered as "What's 'is name"
who's to say?

crawling over asphalt and cement
you can use as many feet as you can get

La Biancuccia

blanched wall, a name scrawled
a dog barking

the sun in the street
looks for a place to lie
gnawing at the earth
like a bone

steel shines white in the sun
assaulting anything with a voice

a fish lies on a table outside
its mouth open
I can hear someone singing
the sun's name

La Stella

light returns –
its myth is a name
that names myths

the name comes from the telling
climbing up over the lips' round horizon

what is said to appear
appears to sound
a sound appearance

what is unknown is believed to be
what is obscured sheds light

in the gathering to hear, the gatherings begin
and the name takes place

La Vinciolina

do not hurry the tale

to where is it she dances and why
does he follow her as she hears her name
on his lips and follows him as he dances
his steps to the tune sprung from
her lips singing his name

do not hurry the tale

a name is a gift lingered over
and through its invocation
a story appears of the telling and the told
through his lips on hers, her lips on his

do not hurry the tale

Afterword

Invenzioni e Stravaganze was inspired by early baroque Italian composers. To various degrees and in various ways, the composers I have chosen move in and out of these poems. I have invested sometimes only part of a poem, sometimes a whole poem, with a composer's music and/or biography. And often times the poems are only about ideas that the facts of a composer's music and life raise. In many ways, the poems are improvisations that riff off the composers I have chosen: the facts of their music and lives, and their and others' words.

The dates following each composer's name denote not the dates of his birth and death but rather the period of his artistic activity, as far as I have been able to determine; the cities named are the cities where the composer was active artistically.

Many of the composers named in these poems seem to have been lost to the general listener of classical music in recent times, but thanks to the early music movement, many of them have been again brought to light. The early baroque saw many experiments in music: the movement from polyphony to monody, the development of instrumental music from being primarily accompaniment for vocal music to an autonomous genre in its own right, and the development of the seconda practica in which the form of vocal music reflected and fit the meaning of the words, as opposed to the prima practica in which the words were made to fit the musical form, if I may be forgiven a gross oversimplification.

The experimentation of the early baroque also included many inventions and extravagances in the forms that musical compositions took. The high baroque's consolidation of form had not yet taken place; this was a period of musical adventurousness. These musical explorations have also inspired *Invenzioni e Stravaganze*. Consequently, there are many types of poems in the series: from call and answer to dramatic monologue, from riddle to sonnet, from story to list to song, and many invented types. In addition, I hope that the subject matter and language of the poems reflect something of the invention found in these early baroque musical compositions. The poems are concerned with various topics, among them: memory, both personal and historical; the movement of love and of music; movement through time; movement through geography; rapture; truth; dialogue; articulation; silence; echoes; song; transfiguration; metamorphosis, identity, naming.

Music and poetry; the connection is important to me. In many ways, the two are identical for me: they both use sound, both take place in time, both seem to move with a fluidity of association at times, both have a sensual dimension to them, both can be an outcry or a whisper and everything between, are articulations of vibrating air, and both are avenues of enlightenment. I tend toward a belief, along with Orpheus (or, rather, what Orpheus dramatizes through his many cultural manifestations) and Hazrat Inayat Khan, that the world comes from sound and vibrations, manifests itself through vibrations, that each being has its own vibrations, that particular beings come into existence through vibration. Whether it's Orpheus travelling down through the levels of the spheres and learning music, which can be taken as a correlative to beings moving as vibrations through the spheres and eventually taking physical forms, or Hazrat Inayat Khan discussing how sound and vibration are the origin of this world and the source from which beings spring, I am fond of this idea of forms and flesh coming from sound and vibration. It rings true to me, if I am allowed the pun. So much of western philosophy is based on the sense of sight; even some of my favourite poets, the Objectivists, for example, have their poetics rooted in sight. But even in the west, there has been a tradition – especially seen in the many versions of the Orpheus story, indeed in the very persistence of that story – in which sound is the stuff of beings, in which sound is the dimension that leads to enlightenment. Beings – and not just humans, but animals and plants too, as both Khan and Orpheus tell and show us – react to music because they are made of vibrations and sound themselves. This is why we dance, why we open our mouths and speak and sing.

AT SOUND

To my Mother and Father

Orpheus and Eurydice

Deserts   *(after Edgar Varese)*

what we do not see, we hear

fugitive notes
wander between rumours
or hover
"threateningly dormant"

what does this woman do
alone in her rooms
wandering between
memory and memory?

how does she grasp the end?

drum in the hallway unseen
she puts her hand through
the water, the mirror

glance touches air to gesture
sleep taps on leaves
hums on the other side of the window
carries an old hand in an old pocket
moves the soil from here to there
the song from silence to sound to silence

she listens to the horizon
page becoming paper

another voice is always there

Orpheus and Eurydice

who enters
is gone at the glance

the beloved cannot be seen

only sound remains in the rock

a suspension, a taciturn dissonance
slips by unrecognized
yet is heard by the ears

slip out of the snake skin
guitar in hand
and there is only the song
to be heard

what the ear holds, seems an echo
what is silent, fills the mind

"a sonorous horizon, an acoustic perspective"

she was there, breathing at your neck

Orpheus and Eurydice

"Every Friday evening we make music
in the Hall of Mirrors."

air rushes through the mouth

sung speech or spoken song

what is past the mirror, the water?

corpus opus
body torn apart
body disappeared

she found her own fingers receding
moving backwards through time
or so quickly forward towards
some end she was breathless to imagine
that the only sign of them was
the stops being played on the flute

Madrigal

"Marked by a line of blood
Encircled in sinuous lips"

where in thought…

how far goes the "quaestio notae"
the searching note?

"the whole of nature is breathing"

melody skin in its shadow
wing at the ear
numb eye

shiver moves through thought
moves through blood
sound at the edge
of note and naught

La Musica

she would have
no bird move in the trees
no wave sound on the shore
no breeze slip past the cheek

so that the story would be told

of how the song rose from dust
quivering on his tongue as he touched her
of how his mind was seized with her
and he could feel her breathing
as he stood there holding her
and of how he knew she was gone
though he stood there holding her
feeling her breathing
that each moment he was touching her
she was gone
and how he realized
this had always been the way
she was always leaving
and he was always singing notes
that died away into the air
she no longer breathed

Orpheus and Eurydice

at silence
speaking overheard
wandering

still at moving
murmur turn

wall writing
charmed
at touch
the letters
the form of the beloved
at the strings
hovering at sound
a gaze
turned neither away
nor towards

approached

Madrigal

bell and stone
ear to thought

tone of
varying degrees

lip to lobe
speaks it out

begs the question
breath to flesh

touch gone
hand to mouth

Orpheus

wisp's will
at ear-reach:
rain rhyme
defines branch
arm's harp
sings passage
through skin
finger held
in the wind
listens to
the beat
hand at strings:
will's wisp

Eurydice

she thinks of him going blind
little by little each year
until he entered the dark
and she became the messenger
between him and the light
attending to his needs
listening to his voice

she thinks of him
gone fully into the dark now
his voice appearing
from time to time –
singing –
a messenger between
her and the dark
between her and him

she thinks of him
a distance at her ear
within her arms –
a breath puzzled
undeciphered –
spoken word
whose letters
have been lost

Eurydice

where is it that you move to?
whose hand is that, probing
the dark before you?
do you recognize
the flagstones behind you?

who is the singer you hear?

"you never know when I'll be around"
who is it you hear walking?

"I was away, but now I'm back"
where are you, when you are here?

when does the ground become a place?
when does the noise become a song?

how many faces have you seen
to see this face as you do?

what happens to the
mirrored face when those
faces are lost to you?

Orpheus and Eurydice

among the flock of grackles at your feet
one is afraid to eat from the bread you throw him

how can you read his movements?

even here, in the dark
you can see that
the scant light
turns his body now green,
now blue, now black
through his movement

they are used to being hunted
and hunting
are brazen, and will draw blood
yet he holds back
and you must cultivate his trust

With the weather warming, the grackles flew northward
in small flocks, a jagged script, each part of their flight
drawing a small line that described a larger arc or circle,
and as they flew, they could be heard chattering.

where do you find him?
a song of feathers
and hair rolled up
mud for eyes

what is it he is saying,
singing, descrying?

Echo

she walks just a little behind herself
through turn and passageway
follows her voice's thread
trying to recognize who is speaking

he walks just a little behind himself
through shadow and blindness
follows his voice's notes
trying to recognize who is singing

where is the thread when it quivers?
the tongue when it sings or speaks?
in what places do seam or song dwell?

Hide and Seek

Flesh a lonely game.
Table and ants: another song.
Glare finishes last, right behind wind.
Little voices, engines.
I've already driven through fall. Never mind,
I have the street and her voice for pockets.

"Beguiling impression of this touching voice"
seems to dream with its eyes open.
Grapes...water. Turn here.
Why limit it to a second death?
There's already enough to tantalize the memory.
Fill me a jar, would you?
A fever wrought anno domini.
A whistling in the sleeves.

The rock, and underneath: the light,
and, of course, the saxophone.
A liver in the beak, a rant.
Nothing here but us blinks, or is it blinds.
A string across the mouth, the tongue a plectrum.
April in the tooth. Herringbone whispers.
"As long as we retain so sweet a memory."
Someone's thrown a rock at the light,
and it's shattered to pieces all over my shoes.
Good, now we can get the hell out of here.

Sun, hand shadows, bits of music,
telephone wires, a stuttering fly.
Water in the glass, light in the throat.
Who coughed?
Tuned air. Dust wearing socks.
We have visited this anthem before.
Is it he or she?
C'mon, you've looked too far
into your own fingerprints.

Hand me my harp. Rondo on
the end of a stick. Allegro vivace.
The sky too passes through the lips.
Dangle that carrot; I have a cane
I can dance with. Toes playing
its stops. Pasacalle. An ankle
disappearing behind a corner.
Voice listening to steps.

Is death a shell game?
The aulos players liven things up.
I'm sorry, but I'm sick of being solemn.
Yes, I am dead, was dead, will be dead.
Who cares at this point?
Whose street are you on anyway?
Police Line Do Not Cross.

I haven't found what isn't said
because I haven't looked for it.
I have no words, no shout, no song,
no shadow, no echo. It's as simple as that.
Within this point that isn't a point, I spin.
I have left no thumbprint behind,
no impression on the bed.
Nothing moves,
except a breath dreaming.

Am I a personality?

"She was a personality before there were personalities."

Each day, history begins anew on the airwaves.

We are shadows. Always were. Hum and spin.

Anonymity wags its tongue at you.

I can't remember anything to say.

She sits in a nursing home and tells you

she doesn't know if she likes working there.

Where have her memories gone off to?

"You never know when I'll be around."

She pushes herself around in a walker
made of plastic piping. You come in
on her stuck in a doorway,
not sure where she is trying to get to,
or is it just the wrong door?
Wheels and chrysanthemums.
Who is he beside you, not there
when I look? Or is it she, you?
Holes are what enable us to pipe a tune.

Nothing beyond what you say.
Don't try to make something else of it.
People's lives are still people's lives.
It's not like a car compensating with skid control.
Hide and seek. Look under the tongue.
I followed her through the memories she forgot.
When the strings are broken, they're broken.
Thread dancing on air.
It's just the voice in the throat.

Songs

toward speak
echo in lacunae

broken language
hand at listening

"people in the family
bring me things to sew"

steel fathom
error in eye

"the mere sound of music"
thread evidence

breath with its stitching
story for fingers

events plucking feathers
cages in the picture

the frame broken
the old man holding a dove

bird strung
through the hand

the drawn line dangling
from the dove's beak

breath threading
migration's windpipe

darkness is a place
to woodshed

street at the back of your hands
wrist time focuses note

ladder slat blinds
cicada's circadian rhythm

"at this name I feel my voice fail me"

        chambered notes

           slip reed

distal bell

              seed name for wakening

song at sound

    barely skin

        spool splinter

    rhythm light uttered

she drinking from letters

        each memory a stutter

    still other

        water's sound

through dark

        ground waits

    stalk slow to sepal

blink rises

        finding stare

            stave ear

word not word

    in each room
                from else

    track upon the breath

charred recognition

        rhythm cleft

sense riddle

    swelling the eyelids

gaze cadence

        his blood

an act of transparency

step remembered

        voices at the ear

    letters and thread

another story at the edge of the fingers

    transparent bone in the silence

        the urgency of their eyelids

    locked against each other

        in order to be with each other

           hours born in the voice

tenuous moment touched

    eluding the gaze

        palpable in the ear

voice, improvisatory

    intoning each moment

he at the back of

    step and turning

        strung limbs

    ghost notes

          on blinds

            she blinks

    remembering

      hums a tune

turns

    to hear

         seed pulse

       thread vibrating

    letter's silence

correspondence

    in colloquy

each the voice

       and the echo

Post Face

"At Sound" was written when my mother was dying, and both she and my father, who had died several years before her, figure in the poems. My mother died shortly after most of the poems were written, and before the editing and re-writing was done. So the piece is basically a requiem for both of my parents.

They and Orpheus and Eurydice interpenetrate and each takes on characteristics of the others. Certain reversals and variations of the Orpheus and Eurydice story occur in the poem. For instance, it was my father who died before my mother, so my father/Orpheus speaks from the darkness. The blindness he experienced towards the end of his life, as well as my mother's memory difficulties in the form of dementia also enter into the poems.

Other figures that move through the series at different times, some by their words, some by reference, are Edgar Varese, Ferrucio Busoni, Claudio Monteverdi, Dino Campana, John Adams, as well as a number of other composers besides Monteverdi who wrote operas based on the Orpheus and Eurydice story, such as Haydn, Gluck, Offenbach, Peri, etc. Books that were an influence on me during the writing of this work include John Block Friedman's *Orpheus in the Middle Ages*, *The Monteverdi Companion* edited by Denis Arnold and Nigel Fortune, and, to a lesser degree, W.K.C. Guthrie's *Orpheus and Greek Religion*. Films that were an influence on the poem include Jean Cocteau's *Orpheus* and Tennessee Williams/Sidney Lumet's *The Fugitive Kind*.

CORRESPONDENCES

"*Those who have scientifically studied the different impressions that are made by sound, have found the clear forms of leaves and flowers and other things of nature, which is proof of the belief held by the ancient people, that the creative force in its first step towards manifestation was audible, and in its next step visible. It also shows that all we see in this objective world, every form, has been constructed by sound and is the phenomenon of sound.*"

Hazrat Inayat Khan

Prefiguration

within the song
are found

both tone and word
and neither

read the strings
the ear listens

to their lines and
the spaces between

tongue clap thrown
hue heard and cried aloud

"Otsu! Play the bamboo flute.
It heals sorrow."

sound enters the bone
created by sound

in a quark, the tiniest
filament hums

string quivering
with its own tune

from here to there
a leap between

coccyx singing
cuckoo

hopping from
wire to neuron

gamut plucked
from the air

swallowed whole
spine timed

bone spun
into existence

listening to the absence
it came from

through the holes
on which it is played

nothing you
can't tell

is there in
what is

said to tell
to be heard

sprig throat
erupted through clay

pitched sound
turning dust

round canal
and cochlea

caught in
releasing lips

Correspondences I

Prelude

rumour of sound
cylinder recordings at the far corners

field research: stillness created by moving about

the mind a musical instrument

"who is this before me?"

a step not there,
to be recognized

La Scala di Mano

(The Guidonian Hand)

five and five
fingers and lines
four spaces face
each listening
finger memory
through the grasp
at the hand's breath
"a place is a site
of the steps"
gamut's grammar
finger's memory
at tip and joint
and beyond
musica ficta
locus pocus
finger fingere
figures memory
tapping the table
grasping the
letter ladder
to remember
not to write
the lines and spaces
of the hand
read or recalled
to sing together
the distance
between notes
as distance

...sofferte onde serene...

(Luigi Nono)

sound remembered
beneath the sound board
within the fingers
recognizable and strange
at the rim of
summoning and leaving
sound excavated
from the hollowed metal
rung or clocked
time within chime
pendulum's skin
water and mud
mix in the sound
sinew silt
at the key's edge
trembling between

Monkery

(Thelonious Monk)

splinter hint
stutters glint
mutter dreams
see saw
scrawl walk
on pedals
stride spans
hand time
between fingers
figure it
out
side plays
the side
ways
time outwitted
become rhythm

Fable

(Ornette Coleman)

tune wand
at brass kilter
bow weaves
one way
to three
reed's rhyme
frees fable's
nursery
to grow
slow time
cries speed
between keys
what ever again
levers riddle
fiddles nape neck
turning tune
to stare

Criss-Cross

(Thelonious Monk)

arm angled
to drum skin
writ rasure recorded
face or efface
incus inscribed

you wander
at sound
at sand
knee joint trickles
through the beat

moment's body
sinks mark
bends through
the touch
the key's resistance

what silence between
you and your family?
what wandering
where you know neither
yourself nor where you are?

who found
at the corner
"imaginary writing"
"alternative to the hand"
syllable anima?

overtones
within the tone
understood
pedal steps
between the notes

the notes between
he argues and chooses
augments and subtracts
between the devil and
the deep blue sea

at sand, at water
the great coat and hat
hum your melody
water's presage
to your oracle

we see
brilliant corners
buds walk
let's call this
criss-cross

evidence appears in notes
she is lost in thought in daylight
he is lost in darkness thinking
think of one played twice
evidence appears in notes

what sound remained
how does the melody
find the fingers
the legs the silence
between the steps?

what will carry you
from here to there
from air to air
through the strings
over the table of memory?

pigeon in the dust
dirty iridescence —
the light pouring
through the bird
it changes

colour to colour
movement to movement
incipient iris
string insomnia's
aural geometry

Tempus Fugue

(Ornette Coleman)

blown tones
tell bell
twixt lip
and ear
impart in
parts times
in time
moments
pass by
and by
equals so
long as
can be
what was
at that
brass ring
grown wider

Yakune

(Taiko Drum Song)

"the sound dancing"
in the chest

deer or calf
skins pounded

leap at the
wood's touch

elm and oak
polish the beat

dancing around
cords and staves

shouting and rolling
on air's skin

the trunk hollowed
to fill the chest

Epodi e Giambi

(Gian Francesco Malipiero)

rain moth's
short hammer
taps grain pace
squeeze box
scratches a spring
upon the roof
fiddle back
flute sings
with the
short foot
shore to
poplar

Mondi Celesti

(Gian Francesco Malipiero)

wander tone
played upon
the step
played upon
tongue, eyes, ears
played upon
sycamore and
sand aster
praise visited
voice to
the lips
note at the
bud point's tip
returned to
when it already
is sounding

Sogno della Cine

(Gianluigi Trovesi)

ghost steps
slumber along
ballad wise
slur wing
skitters sleep
through the
ear canal
littered with
slip notes
frame by frame
feathers flicker
through the
projector's
cat squint

The Way

(Steve Lacy)

bell and gong
gone beyond
what tells
note against note

step echo
that is
note not
echo

Moment to Moment

(Pat Martino)

finger to string
to at to here to
announce a nonce
the time being
each measure
meted out to
meet her or him
generously
moment plucked
and released
instant in stance
upon one after
another to each
hand picked
note by note
to hear hereto
moment to moment
at hand

Motion

(Lee Konitz)

the felt note
understood

the given
worked with

the intention
and act

of playing
one note

after another –
"clear, warm

and positive"
coming from

someplace and
going someplace

each day
trying to

find the
right place

Vibrations in the Air

(Anthony Braxton)

                    slipping particle

                                    ghosting trance

                    slide circular note

            staccato susurrus

        hand over hand

                                    quivering tritone

                    splits script

                rhythm blink

                tongues eyelid

        lips in sync

    spoke glance

                            that as that

            moment in play

                second's way

                    severally each

    beating where

                    breath prints

                vibrate

    on eardrums

                            sounds not

            only sounds

Correspondences II

Prelude

fingers caught
in triple time
corrente's fiddle
claps two to one
other's accent

cyme time:
rhythm split
stem bows or
plucks petals
upon air

air's weight
at horn's ceiling
finger on
pad's scale
measures breath

without light or sound
the bow drawn across the strings
the foot upon the ground
the voice in the air
the string between here and there

with hand set to bough
the bow is seen
the song is heard
the fingers release
leaf and note

◊

bird grass
slip timed
sand shim
sifts rhyme
shifts twig
to skin
thistle spindles
spine tipped
leaf teeth
vines string
trail dust
steps' harp
almost air

◊

snail shelled

       calcerous fruit

dust reversing

     its rhythm

       slips organum's

   shadow chant

        mirror voice

become scarab's

      emergence from

  glass sand

◊

spike stem

      corolla for weed

         ray rising thorn

      shorn step

        hem strand

wall white

      water run voice

        transposes path

arm sheer to thicket

      to forested sound

         force pushing through

      branch being heard

◊

breath upon light

   peer and hum

    lip pitch

     glare ripening

    toward air

   thumb stitch

sheer before

   plucked blinds

    windpipe steers

   through leaves

    sparrow grass

     shutters syrinx

◊

        dust falls

           through stem

seed's pointed

        tip minutely

                profuse

olive lipped

        snake tongue

          muttering earth

        moist margin

              slipped through

◊

tympanic print

        time or sing

           rachis ligature

    between note

        split letter

          at reed

   where feather threads

        pinnate beat

foundling shine

     wonder handling

         spine air

spindle and at

      to meet

◊

rhyme wake

        in whom enters

                palm light walking

          wren room

      along and allow

              spiral apse

shy of roads

      brush tyres tatter

          echo filled with canyon

      bee legend

            immigrant amaryllis

◊

temporal bones
hear fingers

slide along
the stem

reconciling
skin to skin

the seam between
in the instant

silent and
only seen

erased and
only heard

Envoi

split second
snail's pace

place where
sound is written

found correspondences
column to column

scala tympani
scala vestibuli

the entrance
the place of no place

beating its drum
movement become signal

the eyelash hears
the place of tones

through movement
of its body

felt through the waters
en domus – in the house of –

Charonia tritonis
horagai, shankha

shank of the hour's
tritone crossing the waters

blowing shell
hearing trumpet

wing to spire
pinna to pinnacle

cochlea and conch
separated and joined

by a breath
by a sound

speaking mouthless
singing in silence

from which arises
the genesis of what arises

Acknowledgements

"The Way" and "Motion" from *Correspondences*. *Hambone*, Number 20. Fall, 2012.

"Passacaglio" from *Invenzioni e Stravaganze*, and "La Scala di Mano," "Fable," and "Moment to Moment" from *Correspondences*. *OR*. Number Eight. Spring, 2012.

"Trio Sonata" and "Sonata Sonetto" from *Invenzioni e Stravaganze*. *New American Writing*, No. 25. Spring, 2007.

"Altri Istromenti" from *Invenzioni e Stravaganze* and "Deserts" from *At Sound*. *The New Review of Literature*, Volume 4, No. 1. October, 2006.

Four poems from *At Sound*. *Five Fingers Review*, Issue Twenty-One. 2004.

CPSIA information can be obtained at www.ICGtesting.com
Printed in the USA
BVOW022359070313

315004BV00001B/45/P